Pearls of Wisdom

From

The Storm

Bill Snow

ISBN: 1-4033-3446-3 (e-book)
ISBN: 1-4033-3447-1 (Paperback)

This book is printed on acid free paper.

1stBooks – rev. 07/25/02

DEDICATION

This book is dedicated to the congregation
of Buckhall United Methodist Church.
All profits from the sale of this book will be
donated to the Buckhall Building Fund.

TABLE OF CONTENTS

INTRODUCTION

You may find some of these works speak to you or express an idea you wanted to put into words for sometime. Some of the works are inspirational, some are descriptive, and some are just plain humorous. It is my hope you find some of these works of value.

I am no poet. I have not studied poetry, nor have I read much of it. So this collection of works probably is not poetry. The works started when my little church, Buckhall United Methodist, held a fund raiser called "Multiplying Our Talents". In this fund raiser, based on scripture, members were offered an amount of seed money in order to raise more money for the church. My wife, who was the recipient of an attempt at poetry by a young suitor years ago, felt I had a talent for creating poetic verse. She, therefore, convinced me I could make a contribution by writing verse about the project. This I did. Either through politeness or sincerity many people said they liked the work. What's more, I found I enjoyed the challenge of taking a thought and constructing it in a way that was short and pleasant to read.

Some of the works are introduced by the circumstances that caused their creation. I included this to help the reader better understand the purpose of the work.

Every now and then I speak of my injury, or the storm as it's referred to in the title of this book. I was at work one day when a bullet came through the window. The bullet struck me in the back of my neck just below my brain stem leaving me paralyzed from the chin down. Family, friends and my nurses do the typing for me. I greatly appreciate their help in writing these works. I also want to thank my son, Ryan, for his lighthearted artwork. Again, I hope you enjoy reading them.

Bill Snow

Multiplying Our Talents

As stated in the introduction, Multiplying Our Talents was a fund raiser held by our church. It is based on a biblical story told by Christ about a wealthy man who gave three servants talents (money) for investment while he was away on a trip. One of the three men invested his talents and reaped a substantial return. Because of his gain, the wealthy man gave him a position of great responsibility. Likewise, members of our church were offered seed money for investment on various projects to raise money for the building fund. For example, a teenager took the seed money and bought a rake to rake leaves. He then donated the money he made raking leaves to the church's fund raising project. With many people investing their talents in various activities the church was able to raise a considerable amount for its building fund. I wrote the following poem commemorating the event.

Bill Snow

MULTIPLYING OUR TALENTS

The other day pink flamingos appeared in my yard,
Figuring out how they got there wasn't hard.
Someone's talent was to place them there,
And now they charge me to move them elsewhere.

Someone else's talent was to buy a rake—
My yard was covered with leaves for goodness sake.
Before too long the leaves were gone,
And now I could enjoy seeing my lawn.

I didn't know about homes for butterflies,
I saw need for birdhouses and beehives.
But all a butterfly can do is roam,
So here at Buckhall we made butterfly homes.

Every Sunday we were greeted with new treats,
Breads and pies and good things to eat.
Then there were sashes and wreaths and dolls,
And Christmas decorations to deck the halls.

One man's talent was to capture mice
And remove them from your basement for a price.
Another man's talent was to take a landscape timber
And build a snowman you will always remember.

Some went to Church to learn CPR.
Others made Bar-B-Q sauce in a jar.
Crocheting and knitting produced works of art.
While stuffed animals once again captured our heart.

We enjoyed so much the crafts we shared
And being able to show we cared.
The gifts we bought, the funds we raised,
But most of all the friends we made.

Bill Snow

Bad Hair Day, Buckhall, Buckhall Today

Buckhall United Methodist Church is involved in many more activities than just fund raisers. When I began writing these works, it just happened to be fund raisers that provided the initial incentive.

"Bad Hair Day" and "Buckhall" were written as my contribution to a church bazaar. Each work spoke of a certain aspect of life at Buckhall. Even though they speak of Buckhall, I suspect they can apply to many churches throughout America. It was these two poems that convinced me there was pleasure to be found in taking thoughts and putting them on paper in a format that was short and pleasant to read. This challenge led to many similar works.

"Buckhall Today" was the last work I wrote by request for a Buckhall function. The function was a celebration of paying off our mortgage on the last addition to Buckhall Church. We dubbed it the "Mortgage Burning Dinner." This was my contribution to the night's activities.

Bill Snow

BAD HAIR DAY

Here I am standing in front of my closet,
I have absolutely nothing to wear.
At first glance, the closet looks full
But there's nothing for me in there.

Every Sunday my dilemma is the same.
It seems that I cannot find
Just the right outfit to wear
Something that suits me this time.

I really like the way this one looks
But I just wore it last week.
This one over here I wore the week before.
Its something new I seek.

I'll wait on this problem and try another.
What should I do with this hair?
I've tried to style it one hundred ways
I fear people will stare.

Perhaps I shouldn't have stayed up so late
Waiting for my daughter.
Truth is she came home early
But I had to finish reading Potter.

The fact is it doesn't matter what I wear
Or the condition of my hair.
The people at church don't care at all
Because they're the people of Buckhall.

Bill Snow

I'D RATHER BE AT BUCKHALL

It's Sunday morning and sleep fills my eyes,
It's so cozy in bed I don't want to rise.

I speak to God with little fear,
In fact, I can speak with him just fine from here.

I could just lay here all snuggled in my bed,
But these thoughts keep running through my head.

There is a friend at church I would like to see,
He said he needed to talk with me.

The kids could really benefit from Sunday School,
I've been too busy to discuss the golden rule.

In the series of sermons on love, this will be the last,
I know it will be as good as the ones in the past.

The softball team played the other night,
I really want to find out if they did alright.

There's a church picnic, and our committee must meet,
I'll find out when in the Buckhall Beat.

The youth and senior choirs have practiced long,
I find it inspiring as they harmonize in song.
Thank you God for my time in church today,
A time to meet friends; a time to sing and pray.

The church is more than a place to meet with God, I recall.
Its family and friends: It's the people that make Buckhall.

Bill Snow

Buckhall Today

I understand you're looking for a church,
I have a suggestion that may help in your search.

I'll describe Buckhall United Methodist Church as it is today,
And maybe this will help in some sort of way.

There's a small little church upon a hill,
This little church may your desires fulfill.

From the outside the building looks small,
It has no columns or steeples that are tall.

But a church is more than a building of brick or wood,
It's a place where people can relax and worship as they should.

You see at Buckhall people come from near and far,
Not trying to impress, they come as they are.

At Buckhall a large choir, ministers of music or youth you won't find,
Instead you'll meet people who are helpful, genuine and kind.

They volunteer to fulfill many functions on their own time,
Committee members, teachers, counters ask not even for a dime.

Although this church is quite small, there's always something being done,
The softball team, church picnics, pancake breakfasts, people having fun.

Today's Buckhall is more than a building, a place to know God as a means to an end,
Yes, it's a place for worship and fellowship, where everyone's a friend.

Bill Snow

Friends

The following works speak of friends. The first work talks about friends in general. One major lesson I've learned from this experience is never take your friends for granted. Friends are too precious.

The next three works speak of specific friends. I don't believe anyone could feel like a outsider as long as Lee is around. He goes out of his way to make everyone feel welcome. "So You Want To Pitch Softball" starts with some basic truth then is greatly exaggerated. As coach of the Buckhall softball team, Lee did get me on the team and I did pitch. After I was injured Lee took over the job of pitching. As fortune would have it, he ended up catching a softball under his left eye. The wound required several stitches. All I could say to my good friend was, "I told you so."

Not a week goes by that I don't see Bonnie and Judy at least once. They have done everything for me from caring for me while my wife attends a school function to seeing that I have wood for the fireplace to keep me warm.

The following works commemorate these friendships.

Bill Snow

𝓕riends

Try to imagine you have it all,
You're at the top of the heap and feel ten feet tall.

Then try to imagine your life is suddenly changed,
All your possessions, status and wealth have been rearranged.

Now all that was important to you is gone,
All that you wanted to accomplish can't be done.

Your possessions and status you expected to carry you through,
These things you worked hard for now and forever won't help you.

You feel betrayed, deserted and left all alone,
When to your surprise true help comes in another form.

The friends you always took for granted as being around,
Become your strength, a source of comfort, grateful to be found.

You'll find your friends will come to your aid,
They'll expect little of you or ask favors to be repaid.

Instead they'll provide you with inspiration and hope,
And give you a means to work through hard times and cope.

The lesson here is plain and simple to see,
You need not wait for hard times to be,

A good friend to all of those for whom you care,
Never taking for granted the good times you share.

Bill Snow

So You Want To Pitch Softball

We were new to the community and wanted to find a church,
When we met the folks at Buckhall we no longer had to search.

There we met a man whose name was Lee,
To get involved "join the softball team," said he.

Come to practice today, be there at two,
Don't worry about a thing I'll show you what to do.

At two I showed up at the field standing tall,
Lee declared, "You'll be the pitcher," and handed me the ball.

All you have to do is stand on this spot,
And loft the ball softly over that large white dot.

When the dirt is cleared off, that dot becomes home plate,
You'll stand here on your spot where you will have to wait.

Before too long a man with a bat will appear,
He'll stand near home plate right over here.

Wait a minute I thought, let me get this straight,
I stand here patiently then loft the ball over home plate.

The man with the bat will try to hit the ball real hard,
He wants to hit it over the fence into someone's distant yard.

As long as he hits it high I'm safe all day,
But what if he hits it low and I'm in the way?

As I hold the softball it doesn't feel so soft to me,
Standing in front of a well-hit ball isn't where I want to be.

I asked, "Do you have anything that might protect me?"
"Well, we could give you a cup." said Lee.

If it contains a protection potion then fill 'er up.

With a strange look Lee replied, "Its not that kind of cup."

With that he handed me something like I'd never seen before.
Drop this in your pants, and you'll need nothing more.

Just do as I say and you'll be all right,
Stick it in before you pitch, just do it out of sight.

As I held the thing in my hand and shook my head,
"You must be kidding" is all I said.

I don't see where this thing could help at all,
Yea, you'd be the first, most pitchers just catch the ball.

Handing him back the cup I asked, "What poor soul did this last year."
To which Lee replied "I did, boy am I glad you're here."

Happy Birthday Bonnie

God works through special people,
This fact I know.
I also know He is with me,
Wherever I may go.

Yet He relies on these people,
To carry out His will.
To be a comfort to others,
And His word fulfill.

You, Bonnie, are one of these,
I know this to be true.
I'm amazed at the things you do,
But more so at what you're willing to do.

Like building a butterfly house,
Or playing me in a card game,
Caring for me when called upon,
And much more too numerous to name.

I especially enjoy your company,
I know you really care,
You make me feel normal,
Although I'm confined to this chair.

So on this special day, your Birthday,
I have no tangible gifts to give.
I offer you my love and appreciation,
It's yours as long as I live.

My Friend Judy

This poem is about my friend Judy,
You've got to meet her, she's a real cutie.

Perfection is her middle name,
Winning at Uno is her favorite game.

On perfection there can be no doubt,
A flaw in her work she can do without.

At Uno it's time to notify your next of kin,
If you luck up and beat her and she doesn't win.

It's not that she gloats over being a winner,
But to lose at anything just isn't in her.

Her next call to fame is her animal friends,
To feed and care for them she'll go to all ends.

She'll travel many miles 'cause bluebirds need to eat,
Not for plain worms but juicy ones with lots of meat.

She built them a fine palace for a place to live,
Nothing's too good for her animals if it's hers to give.

On weekends she's out and about without fail,
No bargain misses her scrutiny at any yard sale.

She doesn't buy for herself it's her friends who benefit.
You have only to give her a need, when you think of it.

You can search high and low, no finer person will you find,
Than my friend Judy, she's wonderful, loving and kind.

Bill Snow

Tributes To My Friend Ned

The following two works were written for one of the finest men I've ever known, Ned Paes. I met Ned at Buckhall shortly after arriving in Manassas. Ned has the sort of personality that attracts people readily. There was no subject or topic Ned was not conversant and willing to discuss. There was no task in which Ned was unwilling to help. It was Ned who came by the house to keep me company after I was injured.

Illness took Ned home far too soon. I wanted to do something in recognition of our friendship. These two works are a means of letting the world know a truly great man and preserving his memory.

Bill Snow

Have You Met My Friend Ned?

This is a chance for you to greet,
One of the greatest men you'll ever meet.

My friend Ned is an active man,
Who does for others all he can.

His first love is to his family life,
Giving himself to children and wife.

There's more to be written and more to be said.
His family is growing, he's now Grandpa Ned.

Buckhall Church is high on his list.
Sunday school, collection counter, or wherever he could assist.

Of Administrative Council he was president
He led our Church in all they underwent.

His achievements don't stop here,
But have been building year after year.

There is great truth in all that I've said,
So many people have been touched by my friend Ned.

A Prayer for My Friend Ned

Dear God and Father,
I have a special request.
It concerns my friend Ned,
He's one of your best.

Ned is not just a spectator,
But a player on the team.
Working with our youth,
On Christian values and self-esteem.

Though it's not your will,
This we clearly know,
But life has dealt Ned
A very cruel blow.

You never promised believers,
A life free from sorrow,
Or that believing in you
Would assure a better tomorrow.

But in your words,
We find the skills to cope,
And in your love,
There is abundant hope.

Please find it in your heart
To give him your care.
Please show him your love,
And answer my prayer.

Amen

Bill Snow

Have You Thought About...

Shortly after my injury, I began to think about many topics I had once taken for granted. It's much like hearing a sermon. When the last words are spoken, the sermon does not end there, but continues on inside your head as you seek to sort it out. Likewise, I had some topics floating around in my head which plagued me until I was able to write them down in some reasonable fashion. For instance, I always felt memories were good and uplifting. Lying in a bed paralyzed, I realized memories had a downside. Knowing I could not revisit many of the things I had done before, left me feeling somewhat depressed.

In the work, "Those Who Serve", I talk about those who serve leaving their children and wife, implying that only men serve. I fully understand and appreciate the service provided by the women of our country, but I could not get a rhyme to express the thought I wanted to convey, my apologies.

These works address some of those topics. I don't mean for them to be mini-sermons, but they are rather interesting and provide food for thought. I hope you find them enlightening.

Bill Snow

MEMORIES

We're older now, me and my wife,
You might say we're in the fall of our life.

The kids who were here, are now all grown,
And have gone to start lives of their own.

We stay fairly busy with projects to fulfill,
But now and then moments become quiet and still.

Often times it's melodies I long to hear,
That take me back to thoughts of a distant year.

As the music plays it rekindles happy days.
Memories return to me in so many ways.

Home movies and photos have the same effect,
Again memories return after years of neglect.

I look through the photos and breathe a sigh,
As some of the memories bring a tear to my eye.

I wish I could go back but those days are gone,
Now there are only dreams of things I have done.

But the dreams take me back to places I have been before,
To happy times where I am young again once more.

Bill Snow

Listen To The Children

While wandering through the park on a warm fall day,
I soon found myself watching children at play.
This is unusual because I never had the time,
Normally there are tasks required to complete the daily grind.

There were children on teeter-totters, slides and swings,
I studied the equipment and saw many dangerous things.
Some were on the teeter- totters unaware of the dangers, I know,
They were pushing up and down to see how fast it could go.

Then there's the jungle gym, which creates wounds to mend,
Children were pretending it was a castle to defend.
If it were up to me there would be no equipment on which to play,
No place to pretend, only their homes where they'd have to stay.

Next to the playground was a field where the grass was awfully tall,
A little girl was picking wildflowers to decorate her doll.
There was a large pile of leaves someone took the time to rake.
The children were jumping in them; what a mess they did make.

Across a path was a mud puddle people avoided so not to wet a shoe,
The children played in it building dams and rivers, so much to do.
Throughout the playground I watched the children playing hard,
To them the playground was a land of fantasy, the perfect backyard.

As I watched a little longer it dawned on me, trivial faults is all I see,
But the children saw none of the faults that so bother me.
I wonder if we are given children to teach or to learn from,
I believe God loves the children and all they have done.

Enjoy the little things in life, for one day you will find they were the best things.

May there always be mud puddles, playgrounds and all the good life brings. GOD BLESS THE CHILDREN

Those Who Serve

The question, "Why do people serve?" has always baffled me.
The servant was always on the bottom rung throughout history.

Yet there is no social yardstick that can measure,
The value of service, it's a national treasure.

Those who serve must leave their children and wife,
On a moments notice, be prepared to give their life.

It didn't take a war such as "Desert Storm,"
To appreciate sacrifices of patriots in uniform.

They leave their loved ones and head for foreign lands,
To fight an enemy across desert sands.

Emergency workers one day in September,
Their bravery and skill we'll always remember

While we escape from danger and run in fear,
They run towards it and let us know they're here.

May God bless those who serve us with pride,
And may God bless America and stay by her side.

Bill Snow

A Collection of Lighthearted Works

The following works I wrote to amuse myself more than anything else. I would hear of a topic which was ripe with the humorous side of human nature, then work the topic into something concise and easy to read. For instance, after New Year's the media made a big deal about New Year's resolutions. It seemed, 70% of the population made a New Year's resolution to loose weight, so I wrote the work entitled "Why Am I So Plump?"

Another example would be "Looking For A Pet". I saw on TV where a lady dressed in cherry red was walking a poodle which was also in cherry red. I thought of all the ways we spoil our pets. I thought this would make a humorous subject.

Finally, in previous works I talked about the fact that it's people who make up Buckhall Church. I believe this is true of most churches. At Buckhall the softball team epitomizes this fact. Softball games are about 40% sporting events and 60% social events. We enjoy winning but not at the sacrifice of friendships with our own teammates or the opposing team.

"Out Here in Right Field" was based on a story I heard somewhere along the way. I vaguely remember the beginning and the ending, but I had to make up the middle. I feel I was still able to capture the intent of the story. I wanted to preserve it in writing. Everyone is a hero sometime.

I enjoyed writing these works. I hope you enjoy reading them.

Bill Snow

Not Lost, Just Temporarily Disoriented

There I was in Ol' Nelly headed down the road,
Some vegetables, the dog and my wife completed the load.
On a shortcut, I didn't take this way as a rule,
I noticed Ol' Nelly was getting low on fuel.

There was a fence post with a sign advertising beer,
Checking Uncle Fred's instructions, I was to turn here.
The wide paved road slowly narrowed, then turned to dirt,
I refused to admit I was lost, my pride would be hurt.

I turned Ol' Nelly around and started going back,
A keen sense of direction was a trait I didn't lack.
Remember the sun sets in the West advised Uncle Fred,
So I checked its position, the sun was straight overhead.

Turning back on the original road, I saw a welcomed sight,
There down the road a piece was a gas station on the right.
I pulled Ol' Nelly in, got out and filled her up,
Even got a cup of coffee in a styrofoam cup.

"Did you ask for directions?" questioned my dear wife.
"Me, need directions, not on your life."
Knowing we should be heading North was of no help now,
Waiting for the sun to set was not an option somehow.

I traveled down the road looking for a fence post,
The one with the beer sign was what I wanted most.
Finding none, I turned left and drove on...and on,
The road began winding left until it was gone.

So there I found myself bouncing down a dirt road again,
I was at my wit's end when the road met an old friend.
There ahead of me was the road I had been on before,
It lead to the gas station, but fuel I needed no more.

Stopping by the station for a second time,
Got instructions that could lead us to a dime.
Back in Ol' Nelly, I wondered if my wife was friend or foe,
Until she smiled and gently said, "I told you so."

WHAT, ME FORGET?

There on the couch I lay lost in thought,
Dreaming I was in the game that was just fought.
When my wife came to me with a simple task,
To run a quick errand was all she asked.

I had to pick up a few items at the store,
Four things she needed and nothing more.
She suggested I write them down,
Did she not think this mind was sound?

Yes sir, I've got a mind like a steel trap,
Did she think only a balding head was under this cap?
Write them down, yes sir, indeed,
How silly, carrying around a list to read.

On reminders, I admit, I forget now and then,
I'm usually good for about one in ten.
But to remember a list of four,
How easy, I'm heading for the store.

Now that I'm here I can remember just two,
Man I'm in a fix, I don't know what to do.
Perhaps if I wander around a bit.
And stare at some shelves I'll think of it.

Not likely!

Maybe I should come clean and tell my wife,
Sure, and hear about it for the rest of my life.
Perhaps my head really is a cavity filled with mist,
I reckon my wife was right, I should have made a list.

Bill Snow

Bill Snow

Have You Seen My Glasses?

My vision was good so other things concerned me more,
I did not worry about my eyesight becoming poor.

At first I denied I had any cause to worry,
Just because certain objects had become blurry.

My friends all told me it was a sign of getting old,
And I should go see a doctor where eyeglasses are sold.

I opened the phone book and pointed one out,
This is as good as any I said with no doubt.

Don't look into bright objects my mother said,
The doctor shined a light that went clear into my head.

He showed me some letters and called it an eye chart,
But for all I knew it could have been a work of art.

The lines all ran together forming a fuzzy mess,
And each part he pointed to looked no clearer than the rest.

So rather profoundly he announced I couldn't see,
Why do you think I'm here, they're other places I'd rather be.

Into a room filled with glasses he went,
And I could tell right away this is where the big money is spent.

On me he placed a pair of glasses and quoted a price,
I thought that's not so bad, in fact, it's rather nice.

That's only for the lens, you still need the frames,
Then he showed me fancy styles with many brand names.

So I bought an expensive pair that even bend at the rim,
Now if I can only remember where I last put them.

Bill Snow

Why Can't People Be Normal Like Me?

I was reading the local paper today,
I was not surprised at what it had to say.
Once again a man exposed himself at the mall,
Exposing himself to normal people, showing it all.

I was not surprised, it happens all the time,
It wouldn't if people had ideas more like mine.
I'm a normal guy with rational ideas, you see,
I can't understand why people can't be normal like me.

Why can't people just be normal like me?

Take, for instance, people who eat mucky food.
Like liver and onions, it's almost rude.
When cooking, people can't stand the smell of it.
The cook needs air freshener to tone it down a bit.

Why can't people just be normal like me?

Have you ever been watching a football game,
Where a bunch of bare chested men flash their team name?
This may not seem abnormal to you,
But what gets me is the temperature is only 22.

Why can't people just be normal like me?

Then consider the way people drive,
It takes all of your wits just to stay alive.
Especially bad are those who drive slow,
As if they had absolutely no place to go.

You're moving along at a real swift pace,
Normal people might think you're in a race.
Actually it's the flow of traffic I'm trying to follow,
So I stay alert and keep my foot on the throttle.

Why can't people just drive normal like me?

Then there are people who spend lots of money,
On fashions that make them look ridiculously funny.
They're so concerned about what's hot and what's not,
You're sure a mirror is one thing they haven't got.

Have you ever heard of alternative music?
Since it's not really music, I can't use it.
Normal people say it's due to a generation gap.
For that same reason, I'll never get used to rap.

Why can't people just be normal like me?

But if everyone were normal just like me,
There would be no stories or novels, only poetry.
People would refrain from physics, biology and chemistry,
There would be no scientists to fight disease and poverty.

And if everyone were normal just like me,
There would be no one to eat lima beans and broccoli.
Like asparagus and Brussels sprouts, what an awful taste.
So many vegetables would go to waste.

I guess it's a good thing all people aren't normal just like me.

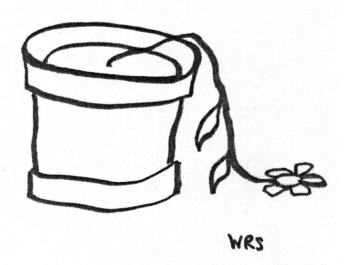

WRS

Bill Snow

Plants Belong Outside

I enjoy indoor plants of every kind,
They're pleasant to look at and ease my mind.

Plants came into my house in many a way,
Mostly gifts, but I couldn't get them to stay.

Their leaves would start drooping before too long,
I read the white tag but something went wrong.

These instructions I followed to the letter,
But the plants, they never got any better.

I gave them to a friend who revived them some way,
She would have them looking better after only a day.

I finally surrendered and faced the truth,
When it came to plants I was just a goof.

They are doing great things with plastic these days,
Synthetic plants look so real in so many ways.

I bought many plants which of plastic are made,
But to my chagrin they're beginning to fade.

Bill Snow

Selective Hearing

I've always been told my hearing's pretty good.
The results of hearing tests come out like they should.

Although my hearing is fine,
I don't seem to hear all the time.

At first I thought this to be a real vice,
But the older I get I find the trait rather nice.

I found with patience and practice on this,
The spoken word was not always heard; ignorant bliss.

When I'm with the guys my hearing is swell,
But when they are passing out chores, I don't hear so well.

So now when my Sweetheart turns to me,
To issue instructions on what is to be.

I turn to her from the couch where I lay,
And politely these words I say.

"What is that you said, My Dear?
I seem to have something caught in my ear."

Bill Snow

OUT HERE IN RIGHT FIELD

I've never been able to catch or run very fast,
In fact when they picked teams, I was always picked last.

But on the church softball team everyone gets to play,
Everyone gets to be a hero, or at least that's what they say.

I found myself here in right field, since I'm kind of slow,
So I'll play in my position, and watch the wildflowers grow.

You see there aren't many lefties who hit it this way,
So I'm safe out here, and still get a chance to play.

I'm lost in my dreams during this championship game,
When you play as I do, every game seems the same.

There are runners advancing, but I don't know the score,
My mind has been wandering, and doing little more.

Everyone is pointing to the sky up above,
So to shield out the sun I held up my glove.

When suddenly to my surprise, into my glove a ball fell,
And everyone in the stands began to cheer and yell.

My friends all surrounded me with back slaps, for what I had done.
The game was now over, and we had won.

To play in right field its important you know,
You've got to be able to run, catch, and throw.

I'm proud to be out here helping my team, and so,
I'll stay here in right field and watch the wildflowers grow.

Bill Snow

Bill Snow

Why Am I So Plump?

When I was young,
I could eat anything I laid my eyes upon.
Now that I'm older,
I can't look at chocolates or a cinnamon bun.

When I was young,
I could lay on the beach looking shapely and thin.
Now that I'm older,
Passersby confuse me for a whale just washed in.

I try to loose weight.
A man on TV said, this can contains a sure diet.
So I thought,
What the heck, it might work. I'll try it.

I bought a case.
If one can was good, three were better.
To my surprise,
I didn't get slimmer, only fatter.

There's an exercise machine,
Which promises a firm stomach and chest.
They must be kidding.
All I'd do is end up in traction, at best.

I'll continue to try,
The mirror tells me to loose weight. I must.
But as for now,
Take me as I am, **adjust**!

Fly On The Wall At Meetings

I'm just an ordinary fly,
Who had an extraordinary day pass by.

The day started like most days do,
Searching garbage cans for some tasty goo.

When flying by some office buildings I could see,
Traveling in my direction was a fly just like me.

I turned toward him to say a friendly "Hi",
When a door opened, there was no longer a fly.

I was in a room filled with people, lights and more,
Too busy for me, I flew to the top floor.

There I found some men holding a meeting,
The man at the end of the table was giving a basic greeting.

I decided to stay and see how these things are done,
It could be interesting to see how meetings are run.

The chairman stated a topic for the meeting to cover,
I landed on the wall so I wouldn't have to hover

One man gave long lectures to hear himself talk,
None dealt with the topic, we wished he would take a walk.

Another man kept bringing up subjects that had been resolved at best,
Unwilling to let go, his solutions didn't pass the common sense test.

Then there was a man who drew pictures, pretending to take notes,
He never did contribute but had some nice pictures of planes and boats.

The chairman offered his solution after a long while,
Everyone agreed with him and nodded with a smile.

Meeting adjourned

Flying down the hall I saw ladies in a bunch,
They were trying to decide where to go for lunch.

They covered many subjects all talking at once,
Only a few of the subjects dealt with where to eat lunch.

Covering a variety of topics from clothes to the weather,
They even covered the men's topic, only their solution was better.

I wondered if they had this meeting on all work days,
At any rate after a long time they went their separate ways.

Meeting adjourned

Flying out the building I saw some kids standing near,
Deciding what to do, their topic was clear.

After about five minutes they headed for the roller rink,
They could teach adults about meetings I think.

Meeting adjourned

As for me, someone just threw out some old fish bait,
Oh, that sweet smell of supper, I can hardly wait.

𝓗𝓪𝓲𝓻, 𝓗𝓮𝓻𝓮 𝓑𝓾𝓽 𝓝𝓸𝓽 𝓣𝓱𝓮𝓻𝓮

When I was young I had plenty of hair,
Some grew here and some grew there.
It all seemed to grow in the right places,
I didn't have the problems this man now faces.

Just the other day I looked in the mirror,
I saw a long curly piece growing from my ear.
I thought to myself, what is it doing there?
That's a strange place to grow a strand of hair.

I even have hair growing from my nose,
What surprises me is how long it grows.
If I kiss a girl on the lips, it tickles my hair,
This causes me to sneeze on the girl and everywhere.

Then as I looked longer, I noticed my eyebrow,
Some distance above it, a hair had grown somehow.
I asked a lady at work, she said, "Just pluck it out."
"That might hurt a bit," I said with a pout.

I noticed most women pluck theirs,
Their eyebrows are free of renegade hairs.
In fact, women are known to shave under their arms,
It's not like it is there to keep them warm.

They remove the hair from their legs too,
Using creams, wax and razors, whatever will do.
Then I found out men shave their chest,
Beats me why, women think hairy ones are best.

It's clear I'm older and growing more hair,
In some really odd places, some here and some there,
But each morning when I wake and look at my bed.
I'm losing the hair from the top of my head!

THE JOGGER

There is a park across the street,
Where every morning joggers meet.
It seems jogging is the thing to do,
For your health you should jog a mile or two.

The President jogs three miles a day,
For me, four miles shouldn't be a long way.
I bought a fancy suit from the store,
I look cool though I haven't jogged before.

I woke early to beat the group out,
Since I wasn't sure what jogging was about.
I even wore matching shoes to look the part,
And headphones I picked up at the supermart.

I heard steps behind me at a steady pace,
I kept my stride, I didn't want to race.
But soon there was a woman by my side,
So I picked up my pace to protect my male pride.

This lasted for about two hundred yards,
I didn't know running could be so hard.
She passed me and was soon out of sight,
She didn't know me, to my delight.

Yard after yard I jogged,
And yard after yard I logged.
I say "yard" because I hadn't made a mile,
I wouldn't reach that mark for awhile.

After a mile I felt a pain in my side,
A friend came along so I caught a ride.
He took me home since it was near,
I went to bed; I'll try again next year.

Bill Snow

Looking for a Pet

You wouldn't believe what just crossed my path,
It looked so funny I couldn't help but laugh.
A purple dog being walked by a lady with purple hair,
It's like they made a matched pair.

I'd like to be one of Aunt Bertha's pets,
They've got it as good as it gets.
If the weather outside is cold,
They wear little sweaters trimmed in gold.

Dog food is sold in great big sacks.
People food has flavor dog food lacks.
Owners mix people food with dog food,
Believing this puts their dog in a happy mood.

It was reported on the news people loose sleep,
Because they sleep with the pets they keep.
The pets wake up several times at night,
Waking their owners who think it's alright.

Dogs make great pets they say,
They're always happy to see you at the end of the day.
You can teach dogs all sorts of tricks,
Like rollover, shake and fetch sticks.

The trouble with dogs is they love to bark,
They're especially fond of barking after dark.
Now tropical fish don't bark at all,
But they're about as playful as a picture on a wall.

Then there are rodents like hamsters and mice,
Two quickly turn to twenty when two would suffice.
Out of the cage they can crawl over you,
But they leave little droppings here and there too.

Cats on the other hand do as they please,
They train their masters and live a life of ease.
Cats like to lay around and soak up the sun,
They'll curl up on your lap after a hard day is done.

Sometimes it's lonely just writing rhymes.
I feel better with companionship at times.
So I'm lonely, there's no reason to fret.
I think I'll go down town and buy a pet.

MOLLY AND LILLY

We have four kids plus two,
Four of the kids act like most kids do.

The other two kids are different from the rest,
But they still consider themselves our kids nonetheless.

One of those kids is furry with floppy ears,
And when crackers are opened, she always hears.

She has a special kind of food Mom buys,
But when we eat she looks at us with big brown eyes.

She doesn't bark or make a sound during our meal,
But the way she looks at you has a special appeal.

Every once in a while a cracker hits the floor,
Quicker than you can say "clean up", it is there no more.

Named Molly she has doggie like features,
Yet has no idea she is not one of the human creatures.

Molly does tricks like most dogs do,
She also does a lot of people things, too.

After the holidays when the kids go their separate ways,
Molly lowers her head, pouts and eats little for days.

She is convinced all visitors come to see her,
When they enter she rolls over so they can rub her fur.

For Molly, she's not much different from the rest of us,
She has trained us to treat her like people so I guess we must.

Then we have a creature we call Lilly,
She has shown us that birds can be really silly.

71

Lilly likes to get out of her cage and sit on your finger,
Once out, she's happy there and wants to linger.

To get out she goes to the corner and flips upside down,
When you walk into the room she chirps and makes a real loud sound.

Her chirps can be loud and annoying of this there is no doubt,
Your choice is to leave the room or take her out.

Once out on you she likes to climb,
She is hunting for jewelry, what she likes to find.

She'll also peck gently on your face,
She'll bite your nose because she thinks it is out of place.

Eventually you have to put her back in the cage,
This makes her mad and she goes into a short rage.

The rage is short because she starts to play,
The games she's chosen leads me to dismay.

In one she lies on her back with her feet sticking up,
Then rolls over and flies up to her feeding cup.

She's not there to eat, just dismantle it,
She puts her head in and pushes it around a bit.

In her cage we put paper rolls to give a place to hide,
She goes in, rolls over and shimmers out the other side.

I thought birds would sit on a perch and sing,
But with Lilly she will try most any new thing.

I'm sure many people have pets like ours,
That can entertain them for hours and hours.

I decided to include these in this book, you see.
So you're not alone in knowing how crazy pets can be.

J. Like Commercials

I must like commercials, I see so many,
Yet I hear there are some shows that don't have any.
But these shows happen only once in awhile,
Anything more would cramp the networks style.

Commercials are necessary or so I'm told,
They try to be clever in hopes their products are sold.
In my condition I can't leave,
So I get to see all they'd have me believe.

Because I see so many of every type and kind,
I conduct surveys and critiques to occupy my mind.
I thought I'd write some of these down,
And tell you some of the things I found.

I've watched older TV shows and the time they take,
Leaves time for only two or three commercials during a break.
Sometimes they would squeeze in an extra and make it four,
Today the average is between eight and ten and often many more.

There are some game shows shown at night,
They are allotted thirty minutes which seems alright.
The game actually takes fifteen minutes to play,
Leaving fifteen minutes for commercials, a bit much, I'd say.

The old commercials would describe what they wanted you to buy,
They would convince you to give their product a try.
I watched an entire commercial aired today,
I couldn't begin to tell you what they had to say.

Hats off to the guy who invented the VCR,
In golf I have to watch twenty nine commercials to see a guy make par.
Commercials are spread thin as the movie begins,
But are packed closely together as the movie ends.

I record movies, golf and other programs too,
Then later fast forward though commercials I don't want to view.
I must admit there are few shows like the Super Bowl,
Where viewing commercials as well as the game is also my goal.

To get the programs we like someone has to pay,
I understand commercials provide the funding, they say.
I know commercial free movies are available for a price,
But I think commercial free TV would be mighty nice.

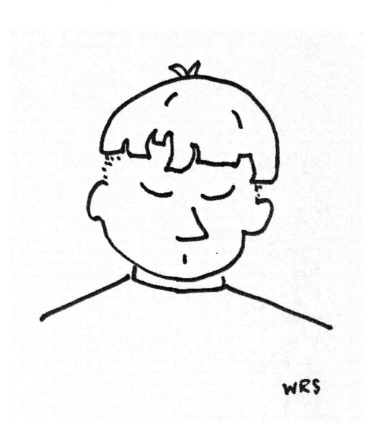

The Haircut Gone Awry

I saw John just the other day,
He looked different in some peculiar way.
There was something odd about him but I couldn't tell,
Maybe it was just that he wasn't feeling too well.

But as John approached me he said he was feeling fine,
He looked funny to me but he looks funny most of the time.
The longer I looked, I was convinced something wasn't right,
Something about his head was canted which made an odd sight.

Then it dawned on me as I looked at his hair,
He must have fallen asleep in the barbers chair.
The barber must have had a day that was slow,
And he must have figured that John had no place to go.

He decided John's hair needed a new style,
So he clipped and cut while John slept awhile.
He cut one side of John's head until he thought it would do,
Following this with the other side, never comparing the two.

He apparently made some adjustment to the second side,
He preferred to cut above the ear making the area nice and wide.
He failed to make the same adjustments as he worked around the head,
I couldn't wait to see the back so "turn around," I said.

John looked puzzled but did as I asked,
Then I saw why the barber did the back side last.
The two sides were uneven, the barber had to connect them.
He could've put a bowl on John's head to get them even..

From the front John looked funny, that was plain to see.
From the back he had a Mohawk that was as ridiculous as could be.
I didn't have the heart to tell him what everyone else would know,
I was just glad hair was one of those things that grow.

Bill Snow

I BUMPED INTO WHAT'S HIS NAME

I bumped into What's His Name at the mall today,
We talked for several minutes because we had so much to say.
At the end of the conversation What's His Name said good-bye,
He used my name, for his name I didn't even try.

I searched the recesses of my mind,
Because he was a good friend of mine.
No matter how hard I looked, I came up blank.
Once again my confidence in remembering names sank.

I thought of many names that might fit,
Rather than try one I said, "Take care, I'll see you in a bit."
I tried every means of remembering names
I've used the alphabet, animals and word games.

No matter what I do, the name won't come.
Makes me feel about two inches tall when talking to someone.
For their name I could apologize and ask
My pride causes me to use this solution last.

To solve this problem I've come up with a plan.
Anyone can do it, even I can.
This is a sure fire way to not forget a name,
We just make all the names in the world the same.

Bill Snow

OH, THOSE TASTY MEALWORMS

This is to tell you about a local craze,
It's quite a business so I know it is more than a phase.

It seems everyone wants bluebirds in their yard,
To attract them doesn't seem very hard.

To attract them you make a place for them to live,
They like mealworms if you have some to give.

Mealworms are not as hard to find as you might think,
They will live anywhere, even in your kitchen sink.

Usually found in the refrigerator to keep cool,
They last a lot longer as a rule.

They've been known to get out and crawl around,
Behind the salad dressing they usually can be found.

You don't buy mealworms in groups of five or ten,
You buy in groups of thousands and share with a friend.

Put them out twice a day and the bluebirds come,
Bluebird watchers say you will always get some.

What happens if the bluebirds stay away?
What would you do with a refrigerator full of worms, anyway?

Just fry them up in vegetable oil,
And slice some potatoes and wrap it in foil.

Who knows, they might make a good meal,
With a French name, people may think they are a good deal.

As for me, I will order my thousand with little fear,
There has got to be a bluebird somewhere around here.

Bill Snow

Why Me Lord?

This was the most difficult work for me to write. It seems from the moment I began to realize I had been seriously injured, I began asking the question, "Why me Lord?" I couldn't understand what happened to the concepts of guardian angels and a benevolent Father. This work was written after hours of study and talking with my dad, a minister, my own minister and many friends. I sincerely believe what I have written is true. I have found comfort in these words. Perhaps if you face difficulties in your life they will come to your aid as they did mine.

.

Bill Snow

Why Me Lord?

As I lay here in bed a host of thoughts fill my head,
I reflect sadly on the life I should have had.

I'm caught up in a world of disbelief,
And wallow in self-pity while caught up in my grief.

I felt I was a good follower trying to do what your book did say,
I asked for good health and your protection as I knelt down to pray.

I always believed tragedy hit the other guy, you see,
I felt I was special and those things wouldn't happen to me.

So you might understand why I believe this can't be,
But as time passes on, my condition is plain to see.

As I reflect on the situation I'm in, my disposition turns to rage,
I had planned to do so much in my life, I am still at an early age.

So why did this tragedy have to strike me now,
What could I have done to deserve this, can you lift it from me somehow?

As I look back on my life it was not free of sin,
If you would take this from me I promise not to behave this way again.

With you I've tried every tactic but there's no change in my estate,
What are you trying to tell me, must I accept my fate?

There is no reason to deny, no cause for anger, I am this way I fear,
For my condition will remain as it is for a time, so where do we go from here?

******

Once again I turn to your book, which I had read,
But this time I paid attention to the promises you said.

I read you never promised me a trouble free life,
One that was free from all turmoil and strife.

Through Christ you said the sun rises on us all,
On the righteous as well as the wicked, rain will fall.

As I read on, it became plain to see,
That there was no point in asking the question "Why me?"

Until now my most important concern was self,
Now I put you above my possessions, status and wealth.

By placing you first in our life we are offered a wonderful gift,
You will give us rest when we are weary and burdens you will
lift.

So "Why me Lord?", because the rain happened to fall my way,
But I know you love me Lord and will be with me everyday.

Make me your servant Lord and care for my soul,
Use me to fulfill your will and once again I will be whole.

In wholeness we find purpose, a reason to try,
Without which there's emptiness as we wait to die.

In your words we find a means to cope,
And in your love, we find Hope.

The Sermon

A serious injury can go a long way in causing one to examine their values. While I was still in rehabilitation, I was visited by my minister, John Hull. At that time I had already begun to assess what had been important to me versus what is now important. These were related to John as four points. He agreed with them and encouraged me to write them down so I could pass them on to others. I went for some time after returning home doing little work on them and probably would have let the whole idea slide into oblivion if it weren't for encouragement from John. He cornered me and asked me to pass these points on to the congregation as a sermon. This I eventually did. It has since been presented to a number of audiences. I pass it along to you here so that you may benefit from a positive consequence of my injury.

Bill Snow

**Sermon delivered to Buckhall
March, 2001**

I want to make four points.

My 1st point:
   On April 9th, 1998, I was hit by a bullet in the neck. I was immediately paralyzed from the neck down.   My friends comforted me while waiting for the ambulance to come. It took approximately five to eight minutes for the ambulances to arrive. Since the bullet severed my spinal cord, I was not breathing during this time. I can remember when I was young and tried holding my breath underwater, I was good for about thirty seconds. This time it was much longer. When the paramedics arrived, I was a dark shade of purple, but I was still alive. Later the paramedics told me they did not expect me to survive to the hospital. Once at the hospital, the story remained the same.

My wife, Eleanor, was in North Carolina and it took them some time to contact her. She was told the doctors would try to keep me alive until she could reach the hospital. She was told, in the best case, I would still be alive, but had suffered significant brain trauma. The doctors had pretty well written me off. What they didn't know was that an entire community had begun to pray. The doctors did not understand the power of prayer. Neither did I.

Up until this point, God, to me, was a concept I was constantly evaluating. I wanted to put Him in a test tube and analyze Him to see if the concept was really true. I couldn't figure out how God fit into the grand scheme of things. I was asking questions which would validate the authenticity of what was being said in the Bible ... who wrote it, when did they write it, what language was it written in, etc. I knew there must be a God, but I couldn't develop my own rational explanation on where God existed, where and how Heaven existed, and how God's grace allowed us to enter Heaven.

It doesn't matter. What does matter is that we believe. The evidence is everywhere. Our small minds will never be able to grasp the wholeness of the Trinity God—the Father, the Son, and the Holy Spirit.

I should not be here. There is not a shred of scientific evidence that explains why I survived. There is though, a community of people, who will, without hesitation, give a rational explanation. They prayed for me, and their prayers were answered with my life. When you pray "for thine is the power and glory forever", listen to what you are praying. The power of God is awesome,—well beyond our understanding. Just look at me and know it exists.

2nd Point:

Life at Kessler Institute for Rehabilitation was strenuous. I shared a room with three other vent patients. It was generally noisy all the hours of the day and rest was difficult. Every minute of the day was filled with either medical maintenance or therapy of some kind. The afternoons were also filled with therapy. I was very fortunate to have Eleanor with me during my stay at Kessler. However, the only semi-private time we had together was about an hour around one o'clock in the afternoon. During this time we would read the many cards sent to us by people from this community, as well as from friends, and friends of friends from all over the world. The cards ranged from inspirational, to humorous. Eleanor would read them to me and they would brighten my whole day. When I was feeling down, they would lift me up. There were times I felt so down, I doubted the value of life as a quadriplegic. My future looked dark because I was thinking about my own welfare. The cards would always bring me back to what was really important. The cards could be counted on for two points. First, they would tell of God's creation, and second, of God's boundless gift to us. I would refocus on those things I thought were lacking, to the gifts God had given me … the greatest of which were wonderful friends and family. In these quiet, still moments with Eleanor, I was able to regain my stability and values. Your cards do count. Send them to people whom are in need, they do make a difference.

3rd Point:

During my stay at Kessler, I often thought of the many things I had planned to do during my life, but now would not be able to do. I thought I would ask God for one day of normal existence. I often thought about what I would do with my one day. At first I thought I'd play golf, or go fishing or play tennis, but I quickly realized this would be a terrible waste of my only day. I thought about the things I really enjoyed; being a part of the softball team, going to church picnics, being with friends, playing tennis with my sons and daughter, going to Bible study and, in general, going to church. These were times of fellowship. In short, I really didn't need a day after all.

What I really enjoy more than anything is being with my family, and being with my friends, and I will still be able to do these things. I cannot understand how anyone can pass up a chance for fellowship, a covered dish supper, a church picnic, a volleyball game, a chance to be with friends. This is what life is all about. I didn't lose the most important aspect of life and for that I'm very, very grateful. The lesson I learned was never to take fellowship for granted. Take advantage of every opportunity you have for fellowship. Your success will not be measured by the number of things you have, if you find yourself in an undesirable situation, your things will not be able to help you. Your friends will. They will come from all corners of the earth. You will be amazed. Your success will be assured through the friends you have made in fellowship. I am grateful for this fact.

4th Point

More than three years have passed since those days I spent at Kessler. I still am not able to breathe on my own and I must have constant nursing care. I am grateful to those who have cared for me, especially my wife, whose life has had to change so drastically, and my children for their love and understanding. I am not supposed to be alive today. All the odds were against it. In the eyes of this humanistic world, I had already been written off. So when I am lifted out of my wheelchair and placed in bed for the night, I thank God for the gift of the day just passed. Have I accomplished anything? Yes, I have lived. My brain, which isn't supposed to work at all, has allowed me to appreciate all that

I am able to see in my field of vision. I have watched the squirrels at play, I have seen the birds eating from their feeders and listened to their song as they serenaded me from the trees over my head. I have enjoyed the abundant growth and beauty of the flower beds my wife and daughter have so carefully planted. Perhaps I have had the pleasure of an opportunity to talk or visit with those I love, friends and family. I have watched and enjoyed the exuberance of my children and their friends during the times they have been able to be at home. Because of our special van, I have shared in the everyday chores most people take for granted—like shopping at the mall or watching the sports events in which my kids are involved. I have had the opportunity to go to church for fellowship with good people and to thank God for His many blessings. Treat each day as a gift. Don't waste it in despair, anger or depression. Yes, life is good, and I praise God for the gift of each new day.

ABOUT THE AUTHOR

Bill Snow graduated from the United States Military Academy at West Point in 1973. He spent twenty-two years serving his country as an officer in the Army. He retired as Chief of Staff, XVIII Airborne Corps Artillery and then went to work on a special military project called Joint Precision Strike. While working on this project, he was shot in the back of the neck and was left a ventilator dependent quadriplegic. He is paralyzed from the chin down. Not wanting to sit indefinitely, he began writing short rhymes about insights and observations gained since the injury.

Bill lives at home in Northern Virginia with his wife, Eleanor. They have four terrific children: Ryan, Matthew, Benjamin and Bethany.